WORLD'S WEIRDEST
BATS

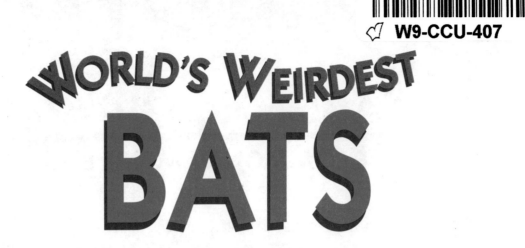

by M. L. Roberts

Consultant: Dr. Nancy B. Simmons, Assistant Curator,
Department of Mammalogy, American Museum of Natural History

WHISTLESTOP ®

Troll

CARE FOR A BITE?

THE COMMON VAMPIRE BAT

Count Dracula and other vampires you see in horror movies or read about in books are just make-believe. But vampire bats are very real!

Vampire bats live in Central and South America. The only item on this bat's menu is blood. Like the vampires in stories, the vampire bat only comes out at night, and it strikes while its victim—usually a pig, a cow, or a chicken—is asleep. When the bat finds a victim, it uses its razor-sharp front teeth to bite the animal on a hairless spot, such as its feet or ears. Then it laps up the blood with its tongue. Delicious!

Vampire bats aren't as scary as they sound. They only bite people if they can get to them easily, and of course people are very careful if they know there are vampire bats around. An animal bitten by a vampire bat won't bleed to death. But the animal might get sick if the bite becomes infected or, worse, if the animal gets rabies from the bat bite.

Bats are great at flying, but the vampire bat is great at walking, too! It can jump on all four legs like a frog, or walk around like a monkey. Better watch your step!

JUST HANGING AROUND

THE EGYPTIAN FRUIT BAT

This picture isn't upside down—the bat is! When it isn't flying, a bat spends almost all its time hanging upside down by its feet. Bats have what is called a *digital lock*. Their strong toes (their *digits*) have sharp, curved claws that can get a grip and then lock around a branch or inside a crack on a cave ceiling. A bat's hold is so powerful that it may not let go even when it is dead!

As you can tell by their name, fruit bats eat fruit. They are part of a group called *megabats,* or *Megachiroptera* (meg-ah-kee-ROP-ter-ah). That's a big word that means "big hand-wing" in Latin.

SILENT FLYER

THE SEROTINE BAT

Birds fly, and so do bats. But a bat's wings are very different from a bird's. In fact, these two animals have hardly anything in common! Bats are the only mammals that can fly. A bat's wings are made of four long fingers and a short thumb, just like a human hand. A bat can move its fingers the same way you can. This lets the bat change the shape of its wings so it can zigzag, dive, and do all sorts of neat tricks. You might say this animal is a real acro*bat*!

The serotine bat shown here lives in Europe. These bats are only about 4.5 inches (11.5 cm) long, but their wings are much larger than their bodies. That helps the bat get plenty of hang time!

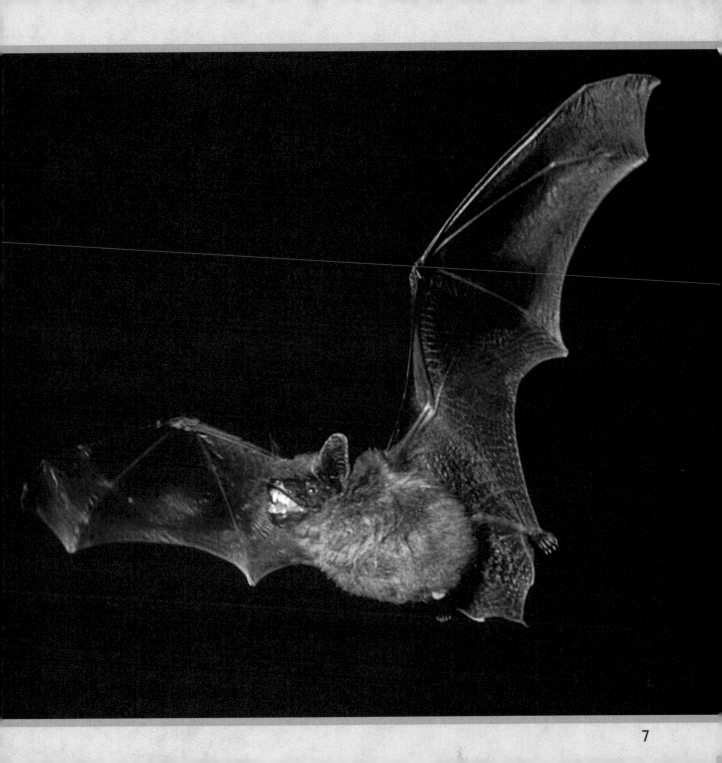

WHAT BIG EARS YOU HAVE!

THE BIG-EARED BAT

This bat is all ears! Because bats fly at night, it is more important for them to hear what's going on than it is to see. So the big-eared bat is perfectly suited for nightlife in the animal world.

Big-eared bats are part of a group called *Microchiroptera* (my-kro-kee-ROP-ter-ah), or "little hand-wing." They are also called *microbats*. Microbats have a special skill called *echolocation* (ek-oh-lo-KAY-shun) that helps them find food—and also explains their huge ears. A bat makes high-pitched squeaking noises as it flies. These sounds strike objects and bounce back to the bat as echoes. By listening to these echoes, the bat can tell exactly where the object is and how fast it is moving. The bat uses this information to tell if the object is a tasty insect or a brick wall. Echolocation is sort of like bat radar!

Most big-eared bats live in the western deserts of the United States, but they can be found in other parts of the country, too. They make their homes in caves. When the weather gets cold, big-eared bats don't *migrate,* or travel to a warmer place. They *hibernate,* or sleep through the winter, inside the cave.

A LONG WINTER'S NAP

THE BIG BROWN BAT

Don't these big brown bats look cozy? They are hibernating. Many bats hibernate. They find a sheltered place, such as the inside of a cave, a hollow tree, or even the attic of a house! Because hibernating bats have to live off fat stored in their bodies, they use the smallest amount of energy they can to stay alive. Even their breathing and heartbeat slow down. A hibernating bat's heart rate can drop from 900 to 20 beats a minute. Talk about lazy!

Big brown bats are one of the largest North American bats, but even they aren't really very big. This bat is about 5 inches (12.7 cm) long and weighs less than half an ounce (about 12 grams).

Most types of female bats give birth to one baby at a time. But the big brown bat often has twins or triplets, and sometimes even quadruplets (four babies)! That's one big bat family!

FUNNY FACE

THE HORSESHOE BAT

Here's a creature that isn't about to win any beauty contests! This bat gets its name from the horseshoe-shaped *nose leaves* on its face. These flaps of skin may look weird, but they are an important part of the bat's echolocation system. As the bat flies, it makes squeaking noises in its throat that are projected through its nose. Those funny-looking nose leaves help direct and focus the sound, so the bat can find its way around in the dark.

Horseshoe bats live in Europe. They weigh only a quarter of an ounce (7 grams). Horseshoe bats are so small, you could fit one in a matchbox!

Can you wiggle your ears? Like all bats, the horseshoe bat can. In fact, it can wiggle each ear separately! That's a neat trick to perform at parties!

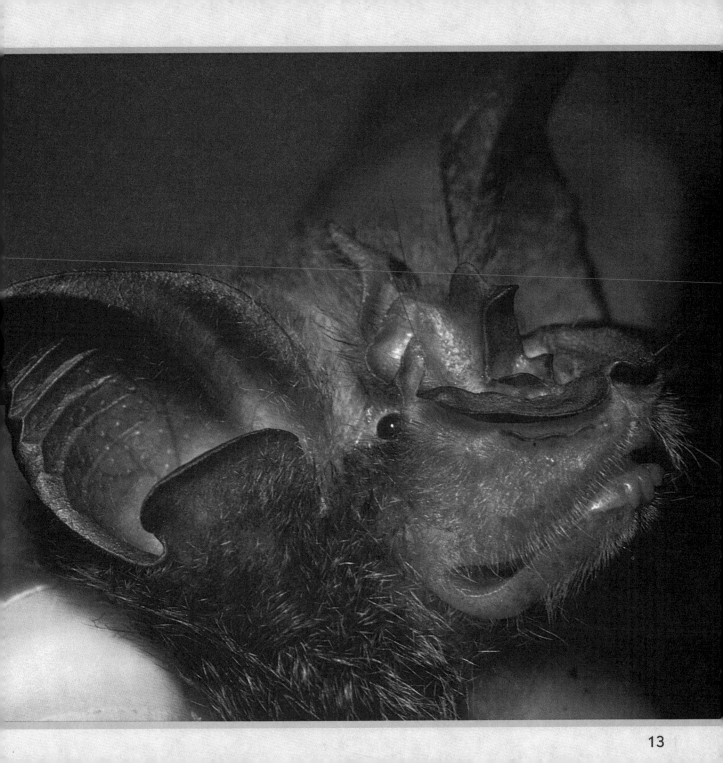

A NOSE FOR FOOD

THE FLYING FOX

Bats that hunt insects use echolocation and their sense of hearing to find tasty treats to eat. But this system isn't essential for bats that eat fruit. Fruit-eating megabats, like the flying fox, use their senses of smell and sight to find their dinner. Because of this, megabats have bigger eyes and longer noses than insect-eating bats. And since it isn't as important for a fruit-eating bat to hear what's going on, its ears are usually small.

The flying fox got its name because its face looks like a fox's. This member of the megabat group is the largest type of bat. Some kinds of flying foxes can weigh more than 2 pounds (1 kg) and have wingspans of more than 5 feet (1.5 m). They don't call them megabats for nothing!

Have you ever heard the expression "blind as a bat"? That's not true of megabats at all. Their eyesight is very good, because they use it to find their food. Even the microbats, which use their sense of hearing to hunt, can see perfectly well.

TINY SLEEPERS

THE PIPISTRELLE BAT

Winter means naptime for the little pipistrelle (PIP-is-trel) bat. Large groups, or *colonies,* of bats find a cave, an attic, or another safe, sheltered spot and hibernate there during the cold winter months. By sleeping close together, the bats can share their body heat to keep warm. But living so close together can cause problems. If one bat has fleas, soon *all* the bats have fleas. That can be an itchy situation!

Pipistrelles are among the smallest bats found in North America and Europe. They weigh only a quarter of an ounce (7 grams) and are just 2.5 inches (6 cm) long. As night approaches, pipistrelles are among the first bats to take flight. Sometimes they even come out before sunset to start hunting for tasty insects to eat.

The pipistrelle in this picture isn't wearing sparkly armor. It's covered with tiny drops of water called *dew.* This often happens to bats that hibernate in caves or other cool, damp places. Because the bat's body is warmer than the air, drops of water form on its coat. This makes for a damp bed, but the bat doesn't mind. In fact, if it wakes up and feels thirsty, the bat can just lick its fur to get a drink!

OUT FOR A SNACK

A NEOTROPICAL FRUIT BAT

This fruit bat is about to chow down on some tasty bananas. Even though fruit bats have sharp teeth and could eat insects, they eat fruit for the same reasons that we do—because it tastes good and is nutritious. The fruit bat looks for soft, ripe fruit to eat. It mashes the fruit in its mouth. Then it swallows the juice and pulp and spits out the rest.

Many farmers hate fruit bats because the bats eat their crops. These farmers try to chase the bats away. Sometimes they even try to kill them. But fruit bats do more good than bad. As they eat and fly, the bats help spread seeds to new places. This helps new plants to grow.

Most fruit bats live in tropical places such as Africa, South America, Asia, and parts of Australia. The warm, wet weather in these parts of the world means that fruit grows all year round—so the fruit bat never has any trouble finding a meal.

IN HIDING

THE HOARY BAT

"**H**oary" is an old-fashioned word for something that is so old, it has turned white. The hoary bat isn't that ancient, but its fur is frosted with white. That's how it got its name.

Like other bats, the hoary bat is active only at night. During the day, it *roosts,* or hangs, under the leaves of trees. These bats blend in so well with the colors of the trees that most people never see them.

Hoary bats are found throughout the United States and southern Canada. They are much larger than most North American bats. When the weather gets too cold, hoary bats migrate south to warmer places.

The hoary bat is the only bat found in Hawaii. No one is really sure how it got there, but some scientists think a storm thousands of years ago blew some bats off course. However they got there, bats are so rare in Hawaii that they are on the list of endangered species. Anyone who hurts a hoary bat in Hawaii can be put in jail for his *bat* crime!

HEIGH-HO SILVER!

THE SILVER-HAIRED BAT

ike the hoary bat, this bat's fur is tipped with silver. Silver-haired bats live all over North America, from the Deep South all the way up into Canada.

Like other microbats, silver-haired bats come out in the early evening, looking for insects to eat. Their favorite foods are mosquitoes and moths. Unlike other bats, the silver-haired bat likes to be by itself. Instead of joining a large colony in a cave, this bat is happy to roost under loose bark on a tree or hide behind a rock. Sometimes these bats even hang out in old woodpecker holes.

Silver-haired bats like to travel. Most of these bats migrate, heading south to warmer places in the winter. Sometimes, if a silver-haired bat gets caught in a storm and is blown off course, it will stop for a rest on a ship out at sea. That's when this frequent flyer might need a map!

CAMPING OUT

A TENT-BUILDING BAT

Most bats roost in caves, mines, buildings, or tree branches. But the tent-building bat has a different home sweet home. This little bat chews holes in the central rib of a big palm leaf, causing the leaf to fold in half. This makes a tent that protects the bat from rain, sun, and wind. And the holes the bat chewed through the leaf are perfect for the bat's claws to hold on to as the bat hangs upside down under the leaf.

Tent-building bats live in Central and South America. They are part of the microbat group, and fruit is their favorite food.

Leaves protect the tent-making bat from rough weather, but they also protect it from *predators,* other animals that might want to eat it. The animals that prey on bats include owls, snakes, raccoons, and even other bats. Just like other animals, bats have to pay attention if they want to stay out of a predator's supper dish!

ONE BIG HAPPY FAMILY

THE CALIFORNIA MYOTIS

As you can tell from its name, this bat lives in California. It can also be found in other parts of the western United States and Canada. These bats, like other members of the *myotis* (my-OH-tis) group, usually live in large colonies. At night they leave their homes in caves or buildings to hunt for insects.

Where do baby bats live? In bat nurseries! When mother bats go out to hunt, they leave their babies, or *pups,* hanging together in large groups. Each mother returns to the roost during the night to feed her pup. She finds her baby by calling out and listening for the baby's squeaky reply. That helps Mama Bat find her little one in the middle of any crowd!

SWOOPING THROUGH THE TREES

THE SPECTACLED FLYING FOX

This big bat gets its name from the white rings around its eyes. They make the bat look like it is wearing spectacles, or glasses.

Like other flying foxes, this bat lives where it is warm all year long. A flying fox comes out at night to snack on fruit. It may travel twenty miles (32 km) to reach a favorite orchard or fruit-tree grove.

What do flying foxes do during the day? Large colonies rest in the jungle, hanging upside down in the trees. If the hot sun gets to be too much, a bat will fan the air with its big wings to cool off. That's what you call bat air-conditioning!

What does a bat do when it gets thirsty? It flies over streams and ponds, slurping up water as it goes. If a bat flies too low, it sometimes makes a surprise splashdown in the water! But there's no need to call the rescue squad. Like other bats, flying foxes are good swimmers. They use their wings as paddles to push themselves through the water.

BUGGIN' OUT

THE LITTLE BROWN BAT

If you don't like mosquitoes, you'll be a big fan of the little brown bat. This furry fellow can catch 150 mosquitoes in 15 minutes. It may eat half its own weight in bugs every night!

A bat has an unusual way of catching its food. It can snag a flying insect in its wing, slide it down to its tail, and then flip the bug into its mouth. Just try eating your dinner this way!

Luckily for us—and unluckily for mosquitoes—little brown bats are the most common bats in North America. These bats are members of the myotis group, and can be found all over the United States and Canada.

Bats are very clean animals. After a night of flying, a bat will comb its fur with its claws. It licks the dust and dirt off its body and wings with its tongue, just like a cat does. That's a tough way to take a bath!

INDEX

Page numbers in **bold** indicate photograph.

Library of Congress Cataloging-in-Publication Data
Roberts, M. L.
World's weirdest bats / by M. L. Roberts.
p.   cm.
Includes index.
Summary: Provides information on different kinds of bats, including the vampire bat, the flying fox, and the California myotis.
ISBN 0-8167-4133-6
1. Bats—Juvenile literature.   [1. Bats.]   I. Title.
QL737.C5R535   1996
599.4—dc20   96-8323

Printed in the United States of America.   ISBN 0-8167-4133-6

10 9 8 7 6 5 4 3 2

Photo credits:
Photos on pages 3 and 19 © by Gary Milburn/Tom Stack & Associates, page 5 © by Thomas Kitchin/Tom Stack & Associates, page 7 © by A. Maywald/The Wildlife Collection, page 9 © by Kolodzie/The Wildlife Collection, pages 11 &17 © by Kerry T. Givens/Tom Stack & Associates, page 13 © by Tim Laman/The Wildlife Collection, page 15 © by Joe McDonald/Tom Stack & Associates, pages 21, 23, and 27 © by Nora & Rick Bowers/The Wildlife Collection, page 25 © by John Giustina/The Wildlife Collection, page 29 © by Roy Toft/Tom Stack & Associates, page 31 © by Wendy Shattil & Rob Rozinski/Tom Stack & Associates.

Cover photo © by Kolodzie, courtesy of The Wildlife Collection.